# My Football Hero: Kylian Mbappe

D1733398

## Learn All About Your Favourite Footballing Star

Rob Green

## Table of Contents

MADE FOR FOOTBALL ...................................................5

REVVING UP, THIS BOY CAN RUN ...........................16

WORLD RECORD MONEY FOR A GENERATIONAL
TALENT ..................................................................24

THE YOUNGEST PLAYER TO DO THIS, THE YOUNGEST
PLAYER TO DO THAT .................................................30

NOT EVEN COVID CAN SLOW DOWN #K7LIAN ..........35

EVERYONE WANTS A PIECE OF THE GOLDEN BOY.....46

KYLIAN MBAPPE OF LES BLEUS .................................55

POWERED BY FOOTBALL ...........................................63

MBAPPE VS. HAALAND ..............................................68

MADRID BOUND? ......................................................82

PERSONAL LIFE..........................................................90

REFERENCES.............................................................101

# MADE FOR FOOTBALL

Kylian Mbappe was already one of the world's top players as a teen, and as he has grown steadily yearly into a man, he has only improved as a player. With his brilliance, speed, and great finishing, Kylian has propelled his clubs and nation to incredible victories and solidified his place in history in only a few years.

It's hard to think that only a few years ago, this boy was going into video game centres to use his favourite star, Cristiano Ronaldo, and now he is playing against him and many more superstars at the highest level of professional football. Becoming a superstar himself.

How did he start?

Mbappe was born six months after France had successfully defended its 1998 World Cup title. Mbappe has always been around football and seems to have been destined to play it his entire life.

Kylian Mbappé was seen as intellectually talented but disruptive when he was a young student at a private Catholic school in Bondy. His childhood heroes were Cristiano Ronaldo, Ronaldo Nazario, and Zinedine Zidane.

He once received Robinho's number 70 shirt as a present from his nanny, who took care of him as a youngster and whose entire family supported AC Milan. Still, Real Madrid has long been his favourite team, which is why it was surprising to everyone when now, at the peak of his football career, he rejected an opportunity to join the Galacticos.

His father once said, "My kid Kylian is passionate about football. All-day long, he plays football. He can also watch four or five football games simultaneously and constantly thinks of new ways to get better at football."

Despite living in the harsh outskirts of Paris, Mbappe has always been ecstatic and enthusiastic about playing football. Mbappe strongly believes in the value of family, friends, and school. However, nothing is more significant to him than football. He continues to study the fundamentals of football every day until he can master it on his own.

His buddies and former teammates had been envious of him since he was a youngster. His previous team's small medals and trophies helped him become known as the future of French football, and these little trophies led him on the path of an illustrious carer.

His parents constantly directed his development. His mother is a former professional handball player, and his father, a working football coach, appeared to be giving their child special training for him to become a professional athlete. They constantly believed in him and are proud of him today. These factors contribute to Mbappe's constant optimism.

Kylian Mbappe has two siblings: Jirès Kembo Ekoko, who is 10 years his senior and was adopted by his father, and Ethan Mbappe, who is seven years his junior.

Mbappe began his professional career at AS Bondy when his father was hired as a coach. Another of his young coaches at AS Bondy, Antonio Riccardi, recalled, "When I first trained him, he was just six years old, and you could tell he was different.

Kylian was considerably more capable than the other kids. He was a superb dribbler and moved faster than the rest. In my fifteen years of teaching here, he was the finest player I've ever seen.

He fit the description of a "crack." Slang for someone who plays like a cheat from a video game.

He transferred to Clairefontaine academy, where he put on several strong displays.

In 2011 Kylian graduated from the Clairefontaine academy. Other well-known players who attended Clairefontaine Academy include Thierry Henry, William Gallas, Balise Matuidi, and Nicholas Anelka.

When it was time to graduate from Clairefontaine, Real Madrid asked Mbappé to practice with their under-12 team and tour the club's facilities before he went to London at 14 to play for Chelsea's young squad against Charlton Athletic after receiving an invitation from Chelsea.

Numerous clubs in France and Spain, including Real Madrid and Valencia, wanted to sign him to a contract due to his remarkable performance. When Mbappe was 11 years old, he also participated in a tryout for the England Club and Chelsea to undergo testing. Just think of how different his story would be if Chelsea held on to him!

Zinedine Zidane had previously invited him to join Real Madrid owing to his amazing skill, but for whatever reason, Mbappe's father preferred Monaco over Madrid to pursue a professional career. Indeed, Mbappe made history by starting his first match for Monaco as the youngest player to do it. According to reports, Mbappe has been a member of Monaco's roster since he was 16 years and 347 days old.

He surpassed Thierry Henry's record, who made his debut for Monaco at the age of 17, 14 days. Thierry Henry would never have imagined that a 5-year-old child he once took pictures with would one day beat his record in Monaco and become the best youngest player.

Henry said, "He was a decent and quiet youngster when I first met him when he was a little child. He was mentioned frequently for his enthusiasm. Football might help him alter a lot of things."

Mbappe asserted that his encounter with his hero at the Real Madrid Training Camp changed his life. He is motivated by Ronaldo. However, he must be himself now since the future of international football rests on his shoulders.

Bacary Sagna said, "Mbappe is a talented athlete. I'm reminded of Thierry Henry by him. He is still young and will continue to win championships throughout his career. Arsene Wenger said, had this to say about him, "There won't be another Thierry Henry for me. However, given his talent, it would be easy for him to outperform Thierry Henry.

# REVVING UP, THIS BOY CAN RUN

Leonardo Jardim recruited Mbappé in October 2015 to be a staple in Monaco's B-team, but after just three weeks, he was promoted to the first team due to his level of talent and maturity. He replaced Fábio Coentrao after 88 minutes of a 1-1 Ligue 1 home tie against Caen two months later, on December 2, 2015.

At the age of 17 years and 62 days, Mbappé became the youngest first-team striker in Monaco history on February 20, 2016, when he scored a stoppage-time goal in a 3-1 home victory against Troyes, unseating Henry in the process. Mbappé committed to Monaco for the duration of his first professional contract; the teenager signed a three-year term on March 6, 2016.

Vadim Vasilyev, vice-president of AS Monaco, who was instrumental in getting Kylian Mbappé to sign his first professional contract with the Ligue 1 team, said in an interview with CNN that he had recognized Mbappé as a "phenomenon" from an early age.

The first hat-trick scored by a Monaco player in the tournament since Sonny Anderson in 1997 came from Mbappé on December 14, 2016, in a 7-0 defeat of Rennes in the Coupe de la Ligue round of 16 at the Stade Louis II, at this point, defenders were already becoming wary of this little Monaco forward.

At 18 years and two months old, Mbappé became the youngest player to score a Ligue 1 hat-trick since Jérémy Ménez accomplished it for Sochaux back in 2005 when he scored the first hat-trick of his Ligue 1 career in the 5-0 home victory against Metz on February 11, 2017.

In the round of 16 first leg match against Manchester City on February 21, Mbappé scored Monaco's second goal in the 40th minute with a half-volley after receiving Fabinho's long ball over the opposition's back line. It was his first-ever UEFA Europa League or UEFA Champions League goal, and he became the second-youngest French scorer in UEFA Champions League history behind Karim Benzema. Monaco lost 5-3.

On March 5, Mbappé scored twice in the first half of his team's 4-0 Ligue 1 victory over Nantes, giving him 10 goals overall and making him the youngest player in the previous 30 years to reach that milestone.

In just 822 minutes of Ligue 1 play, his two goals against Nantes on March 5 lifted his 2016–17 season total to 9 Ligue 1 goals and 5 Ligue 1 assists. His eighth Ligue 1 goal in his last four starts came on March 11 in a 2-1 Ligue 1 home victory against Bordeaux.

In the eighth minute of Monaco's 3-1 victory over Manchester City (aggregate score 6-6) in the UEFA Champions League round of 16-second leg at the Stade Louis II on March 15, he made it 1-0 for Monaco by converting Bernardo Silva's close-range cross. Monaco advanced to the quarterfinals based on away goals.

Mbappé continued his stellar performances each month, scoring twice as Monaco defeated Borussia Dortmund 3-2 in the away leg of the quarterfinal match after winning a penalty.

Mbappé scored the game's first goal in the second leg, and Monaco won 3-1 to progress to the semifinals. On the whole, Juventus defeated Monaco 4-1 to remove them from the Champions League, with Mbappé scoring the lone goal for Monaco in the second leg. As Monaco won the Ligue 1 championship, Mbappé finished the 2016–17 campaign with 26 goals from 44 games across all competitions. Simply superb!

Radamel Falcao, a fellow striker at Monaco, had a major influence on Mbappé during the season. Falcao gave Mbappé the freedom to express himself and taught him how to be "cool" and "serene" while playing; qualities Mbappé said he lacked.

Mbappe told UEFA in his maiden season, "I believe I am the luckiest player in our group because I get to play with a quality striker like Radamel at the beginning of my career. He has scored a tremendous amount of goals and left his imprint on the game's history.

Because it was my first start, the away leg of the Manchester City match was my particular favourite. I remember hearing the music as we came out onto the field, and it was quite fantastic. That was a really enjoyable experience for me."

# WORLD RECORD MONEY FOR A

# GENERATIONAL TALENT

Owing largely to his exceptional performances, Paris Saint-Germain confirmed the loan acquisition of Mbappé from Monaco on August 31, 2017.

Zidane was not assuring Mbappé a starting berth at Real Madrid, fresh from their 12th Champions League title with an attacking three of Karim Benzema, Gareth Bale, and Cristiano Ronaldo in the summer; Unai Emery, the then coach Paris gave a persuasive speech at the Mbappés' house, that was rousing enough to convince the family to take a short trip to the country's capital rather than flying all the way to Spain.

Luis Ferrer, a PSG scout, stated to Le Parisien: "I recall how capable and powerful Unai was. He vowed to play with Kylian and kept his promise. Even if Kylian wasn't completely prepared for a Champions League match, Unai decided to play him. I once returned to Paris around 10:30 p.m. Antero [Henrique, PSG sporting director] was astonished that I hadn't stayed in the south when I contacted him to give him an update when I got there. I boarded the first aircraft at six o'clock the next morning. I rang the Mbappés' doorbell with croissants two hours later."

He said, "Compared to Real Madrid, we had to work twice as hard. We visited his home to meet him and pitch his parents our concept. We had to do a lot of effort to convince him that we genuinely desired him and would value him."

With the World Cup only a year away, Mbappé sought out a famous club where he could be certain of a starting position. He became the most expensive adolescent ever, the most expensive move in a domestic league, and maybe the second most expensive player, behind teammate Neymar, with the rumoured €145 million necessary for a later complete transfer of €35 million in add-ons. When he arrived in the French capital, the number 29 jersey was given to him.

Mbappé didn't waste any time getting comfortable and scored on his Ligue 1 debut on September 8 in a 5-1 victory against Metz, when Benoît Assou-Ekotto was sent after tripping him up. Four days later, in a 5-0 away loss against Celtic in the UEFA Champions League group stage, Mbappé scored his first goal for Les Parisiens.

In PSG's 3-0 win over Bayern Munich in the second group match of the Champions League, he was instrumental in setting up goals for Neymar and Edinson Cavani. For Neymar's goal, he used a feint to take off a defender.

At 18 years and 11 months, Mbappé became the youngest player to achieve the 10-goal mark in the Champions League; he did this on December 6 in a 3-1 loss to Bayern Munich. On May 8, 2018, after winning his first league championship with the team, Mbappé participated in PSG's 2-0 victory over Les Herbiers to win the 2017–18 Coupe de France.

# THE YOUNGEST PLAYER TO DO THIS, THE YOUNGEST PLAYER TO DO THAT

Mbappé received the number 7 shirt from PSG in July 2018, assuming former teammate Lucas Moura's position after the forward moved to Tottenham. #K7LIAN was created in response to the new number. Mbappé declared: "I keep working to advance on the field, and I believe changing my number was the appropriate move for me. It kind of acts as an affirmation. A lot of greats have donned the renowned No. 7 jersey. I'm hoping I can do this number justice on the field."

And boy did he do justice!

Mbappé scored twice in the final ten minutes of his first game of the year, a 3-1 victory for PSG over Guingamp in Ligue 1. The front three of Mbappé, Cavani, and Neymar scored in the league match that followed, defeating Angers 3-1 at home, with Mbappé scoring on a volley and setting up Neymar for the third goal. He assisted and scored a 4-2 victory against Nîmes on September 1st. Still, in stoppage time, he was sent for the first time in his career after pushing Téji Savanier in revenge for a late challenge from behind in which Savanier was also dismissed.

After the game, Mbappé spoke to the media about being dismissed "If I had a second opportunity, I would proceed in the same manner. I apologize to everyone and the fans, but I will not put up with this kind of behaviour." Mbappé became the youngest player (19 years and 9 months) to score four goals in a single game in Ligue 1 during the previous 45 seasons on October 8 when he scored four goals in only 13 minutes of play in a 5-0 home victory over Lyon. Mbappé won the Kopa Trophy, given by France Football to the finest player under the age of 21, for the first time on December 3.

In a 9-0 victory over Guingamp on January 19, 2019, Mbappé was one of two players — the other, Cavani — to score a hat trick, shattering a PSG record from the previous campaign. He contributed a goal to a 2-0 victory over Manchester United on February 12 at Old Trafford in the round of 16. He reached his 50th goal for the team on March 2 by scoring twice in a 2-1 away victory over Caen. On March 6, PSG fell to Manchester United 3-1 at home and was eliminated from the Champions League based on the away goals rule.

He scored three goals in a 3-1 victory over Monaco on April 21 to record his first goals against his previous team. With Mbappé earning Player of the Year and ending the season with the most goals (33), PSG won the Ligue 1 and became the overall champions.

# NOT EVEN COVID CAN SLOW

# DOWN #K7LIAN

Mbappé won the 2019 Trophée des Champions on August 3 after scoring in a 2-1 victory over Rennes. This was his first championship of the 2019–20 campaign. On August 11, he scored once more as PSG defeated Nîmes 3-0 at home in the team's opening Ligue 1 game of the year. At the age of 20 years and 306 days, he became the youngest player ever to score at least 15 goals in the Champions League when he came off the bench and scored a flawless hat-trick in a 5-0 away victory against Belgian team Club Brugge on October 22.

After the season was cancelled due to the COVID-19 pandemic, PSG won Ligue 1 on May 1, 2020. At the time of the League's premature suspension, PSG was in the first position with a twelve-point advantage over second-place Marseille. With Wissam Ben Yedder of Monaco, Mbappé concluded the 2019–20 campaign with 18 goals, which tied for the most in Ligue 1. Mbappé was ranked as the leading scorer because of his higher goal-per-game ratio.

Mbappé suffered an injury on July 24, 2020, during the 2020 Coupe de France Final against Saint-Étienne, which PSG won 1-0. However, Mbappé could not participate in the 2020 Coupe de la Ligue Final, which PSG eventually won, completing a domestic triple.

On August 12, she made a comeback in the Champions League quarterfinal encounter against Atalanta, entering as a substitute and helping Choupo-Moting score the game-winning goal in stoppage time. Bayern Munich defeated PSG 1-0 in the final of the Champions League on August 23.

2020 was a weird year for a lot of people all over the world, and most players suffered huge drops in form while playing through the pandemic. It was worse when the player got the illness, but Mbappe, through his perseverance, was able to change that narrative.

After getting COVID-19 while playing for the France national team, Mbappé was forced to miss the season's first three games. On September 20, 2020, he made his comeback and scored a penalty kick in a 3-0 victory away to Nice. On October 28, Mbappé assisted on both of Moise Kean's goals in a 2-0 win over Istanbul Başakşehir in the Champions League group stage.

By doing so, he amassed more than fourteen assists throughout the four seasons, making him the player with the most assists in the tournament since the competition's start in 2017–18. On December 5, Mbappé scored his 100th goal for PSG against Montpellier in a Ligue 1 game, becoming only the sixth player to accomplish the record for the Parisian club.

Mbappé scored his first two goals of the European season in his team's last Champions League group encounter against Başakşehir, and PSG triumphed 5-1 to win the group and go to the knockout round.

He also scored 20 goals at the age of 20 (although this record would then be surpassed later in the same season by Erling Haaland).

In PSG's 4-1 round of 16 victory at the Camp Nou on February 16, 2021, Mbappé became just the third player, after Faustino Asprilla and Andriy Shevchenko, to score a Champions League hat-trick against Barcelona. With his hat-trick, Mbappé also surpassed Pauleta's 109 goals, moving to third place on PSG's all-time scoring list behind only Cavani (200 goals) and Zlatan Ibrahimovi (156 goals).

Mbappé became the first player to record five back-to-back goals in a single Ligue 1 season on February 27 when he scored twice in a 4-0 away victory against Dijon. Mbappé scored from the penalty spot in a 1-1 draw at Parc de Princes in the second leg against Barcelona on March 10 to help his team move to the quarterfinals 5-2 overall. Mbappé surpassed rival Lionel Messi to score his 25th Champions League goal on a penalty kick. Mbappé became the first player to score four goals against Barcelona in a single Champions League season in addition to his hat-trick from the first leg.

The night did not get off to a good start for PSG as they fell after a Lionel Messi penalty in the 27th minute. Then, as PSG mercilessly exposed the hosts, Messi, one of the greatest players of all time, was outperformed on his home field by the young Kylian Mbappe.

Mbappe turned the game around, dancing past Clement Lenglet to get the equalizer and then stroking in from 10 yards. Ligue 1 champions Marseille took control of the match when on-loan Everton forward Moise Kean headed unopposed at the far post.

Barca was trying to get one back when they were caught on the counter-attack, and Mbappe curled in the game-winning goal with his third.

Mbappé followed this up by scoring twice as PSG defeated Bayern Munich 3-2 in the first leg of their Champions League quarterfinal matchup on April 7. This was PSG's first victory in Munich since 1994. He missed the second leg because of a calf injury, and PSG later advanced to the semi-finals before being defeated by Manchester City.

In a 4-0 league victory over Reims on May 17, Mbappé scored his 40th goal of the year, making this his most productive campaign to date and the first time in his career to reach the 40-goal plateau. Three days later, Mbappé helped his old team PSG defeat Monaco 2-0 in the Coupe de France Final, giving PSG their first significant championship.

It was the first time in Mbappé's career that he did not win Ligue 1 after four straight victories.

He finished the Ligue 1 season with 27 goals, becoming the league's leading scorer for the third straight year. PSG did win the league.

Mbappé was named to the Ligue 1 Team of the Season and won the Player of the Year award at the end of the campaign.

# EVERYONE WANTS A PIECE OF THE GOLDEN BOY

Before Paris Saint-Germain's home opener against Strasbourg on August 14, 2021, Mbappé was jeered by the crowd at Parc des Princes after rumours that he wanted to join the Spanish club Real Madrid. His old love for Real Madrid and the money that the Galacticos control led fans to believe their star man was leaving the Parc des Princes.

The Parisians won the game 4-2; Mbappé assisted in the creation of three of those goals. Six days later, in a 4-2 victory away from home against Brest, he scored his first goal of the year.

Lionel Messi made his PSG debut in the next game against Reims on August 29, and the Rouge-et-Bleu won 2-0 courtesy of two goals from Mbappé.

At the City of Manchester Stadium on November 24, Mbappé scored in a 2-1 Champions League loss to Manchester City. At home, he contributed two goals to a 4-1 Champions League victory over Club Brugge on December 7.

He became the youngest player in the competition's history to reach this milestone with the goals, which were his 30th and 31st in the Champions League.

Mbappé scored twice against Monaco on December 12, 2021, to help PSG achieve a century of league goals.

He became the youngest player to reach 100 goals for a single side in the French premier division since Opta started keeping track of statistics in the 1950–51 season at 22 years and 357 days. Mbappé's first hat-trick of the year came on January 3, 2022, in a 4-0 Coupe de France victory over Vannes.

On February 11, he beat Rennes 1-0 in the league with a goal in stoppage time. Four days later, he defeated Real Madrid 1-0 in the first leg of the Round of 16 in the Champions League. The second-highest scorer in Paris Saint-Germain history, he added another goal in the return leg, but his club was eliminated after a 3-1 loss at the Santiago Bernabéu Stadium.

Despite rumours of a potential transfer to Real Madrid, Mbappé extended his contract with PSG on May 21, 2022, keeping him there until 2025. This caused La Liga authorities to protest against UEFA about PSG's accumulated losses in prior years. Mbappé phoned Florentino Pérez, the president of Real Madrid, and informed him that he would not be joining the team.

The financial terms of Mbappé's contract, according to Sky Sports, include a monthly salary of £4 million, making him the highest-paid footballer in the world. Additionally, Mbappé and PSG received a signing-on bonus of £100 million.

Mbappe also gets privileges as he has a say in the players the team decides to buy and sell and some other decisions the club would make during his stay at the club. Giving him almost managerial-level rights at the team, much like Lebron James and the Lakers.

Mbappé finished the season with 28 goals to be the top scorer for the fourth consecutive season. He scored a hat-trick in a 5-0 win against Metz in the hours following his contract extension.

He became just the third player to lead Ligue 1 in scoring four straight seasons. Mbappé finished the season with 17 assists, making him the first player in Ligue 1 history to hold both the top-scoring and assist positions.

After Kylian announced his re-signing with Paris, Real Madrid president Florentino Perez expressed his hurt by saying, "Real Madrid will always try to have the finest players, but today Mbappé is already forgotten." In a letter to his La Liga colleague, Ligue 1 President Vincent La Brune made the following claims: "Your criticisms of Ligue 1, one of our teams Paris St. Germain, and one of our players, Kylian Mbappe, are based on your perceptions of the league's financial instability and competitive imbalance, which you frequently blame on those organizations. It is intolerable and demonstrably wrong that you consistently and openly oppose Ligue 1 on this issue and disparage our league and clubs.

Real Madrid and Barcelona, two of your clubs, have shattered several records in the last ten years. These two teams have smashed the record for transfer fees six times.

According to player pay, two of the highest-paid footballers in the world are now sitting on the bench of Real Madrid. Despite the European Court of Justice's decision that Real Madrid and Barcelona benefited from unlawful state aid, Barcelona is said to have a debt level of €1.5 billion."

# KYLIAN MBAPPE OF LES BLEUS

Mbappé capped a strong debut senior season at Monaco by scoring five goals for France as they won the tournament. The striker nearly single-handedly secured France's place in the 2016 UEFA European Under-19 Championship final with a brilliant performance in their 3-1 victory against Portugal in the semi-finals. In March 2017, Mbappé received his first call-up to the France senior team in preparation for games against Spain and Luxembourg.

On March 25 against the former team, he made his debut after replacing Dimitri Payet in the 78th minute of a 3-1 away victory in the 2018 FIFA World Cup qualification round. At 18 years, three months, and five days old, he overtook Maryan Wisniewski as the second-youngest player to ever play for France. In a World Cup qualifying game against the Netherlands on August 31, 2017, Mbappé scored his first goal for France at the senior level. In a friendly match against Russia in March 2018, he scored twice.

Mbappé was added to the France team on May 17, 2018, in preparation for the 2018 World Cup in Russia. He scored his first World Cup goal on June 21, 2018, as France defeated Peru 1-0 in Group C. At 19, he was the youngest French goal scorer in World Cup history. He was the game player in a 4-3 victory over Argentina on June 30, 2018, scoring twice and drawing a foul in the penalty area, leading to Antoine Griezmann's initial penalty kick.

After Pelé in 1958, Mbappé was the second youngster to score two goals in a World Cup game. In a post-game press conference, Mbappé said: "Let's put things in context - Pelé is in another league. It's flattering to be the second one after Pelé." Mbappé scored a 25-yard goal against Croatia on July 15 in the 2018 World Cup Final, in which France won 4-2. Mbappé's 100th career goal came on June 11, 2019, during a 4-0 away victory against Andorra in Euro 2020.

Mbappé scored the lone goal for France in a 1-0 UEFA Nations League victory over Sweden on September 5, 2020. However, he tested positive for COVID-19 two days after the game. On October 7, 2020, he returned to action for France in a 7-1 victory against Ukraine, a game in which he scored one goal and provided an assist.

A week later, he scored the game-winning goal in a 2-1 victory over Croatia. France won their Nations League group, advancing to the UEFA Nations League Finals in 2021.

The coronavirus outbreak caused UEFA Euro 2020 to be postponed for a year.

Mbappé received his call-up for the France team for UEFA Euro 2020, his second big international competition, on May 18, 2021. He participated in a group stage encounter against Germany on June 15, scored one goal, and subsequently assisted another goal, both of which were ultimately determined to be offside. He assisted Karim Benzema with his first goal during France's round of 16 encounters against Switzerland on June 28. A penalty shootout was necessary to decide the match after a 3-3 tie; Mbappé could not convert the crucial fifth penalty, resulting in France's elimination from the competition. Mbappé failed to score in any of France's four tournament games.

On October 7, 2021, Mbappé assisted Benzema and then scored a goal from the penalty spot to help France come from behind and overcome Belgium 3-2 in the Nations League semi-final. Mbappé, who was only 22 years and 9.5 months old, had his 50th appearance for Les Bleus in this game. Three days later, in the championship game, he again assisted Benzema to equal the score and then scored the game-winning goal to help France defeat Spain 2-1 to win the championship for the first time. Mbappé won the "Alipay Top Scorer Trophy" for the Nations League Finals with two goals and two assists, earning him the Golden Boot.

On November 13, Mbappé earned his first goal in the 2022 World Cup qualifying matches, a fantastic hat-trick (4 goals), as France defeated Kazakhstan 8-0 to secure their spot in Qatar 2022. Mbappé's super hat-trick was his first for his nation and the first competitive hat-trick achieved for France since Dominique Rocheteau in 1985. It comprised a 32-minute first-half hat-trick. In France's last World Cup qualifying match, a 2-0 victory over Finland, three days later, Mbappé scored and assisted Benzema once more.

# POWERED BY FOOTBALL

Mbappe's ball control is comparable to a skilled salsa dancer. Each stride has an added bounce. He's already crossed the field twice.

The PSG crowd starts to build as the fans' drums beat. Nitrous starts to flow. Mbappe uses a salsa routine to go past three defenders, using the ball as his dancing partner as he makes quick, sharp bursts through the defence. Mbappe claims, "I play on instinct." "I feel like I have to let something out on my heart." Kids in Bondy gave him the nickname Beep-Beep because of his quickness and resemblance to the Road Runner from Looney Tunes.

In addition to being likened to Pelé in the media, his brilliance and brash performances for France in the 2018 World Cup contributed to this. Mbappé is a skilled attacker who can play on either flank because of his talent with both feet. He frequently plays as a winger. Due to his vision, he can create opportunities and assist teammates from the right while also cutting into the centre from the left flank with his better right foot.

Due to his poise, accuracy, and eye for goal, he can also play as the main striker in the centre of the field. In addition to being a highly-skilled player, Mbappé is renowned for his excellent dribbling skills, explosive acceleration, agility, quick feet, and creativity when in possession of the ball, as evidenced by his use of complex feints, such as step overs or abrupt changes in pace or direction to outwit opponents in one-on-one situations. Despite having a tall, slender build, he plays sports and is physically gifted.

Along with his technical abilities, Mbappé is admired for his exceptional pace and close ball control while dribbling quickly, as well as for his superb mobility, tactical understanding, and capacity to outwit defenders by making incisive runs into open spaces both on and off the ball. He can weaken opponents' defences by timing his runs and poses a serious attacking threat during counterattacks. Nicolas Anelka, a former France international, claimed in April 2017 that Mbappé has the traits of a world-class player and that his ability to rush at defences reminded him of Ronaldo from the 1996 Olympics.

Stefan de Vrij, a central defender for Inter Milan and the Netherlands, chose Kylian Mbappé as his toughest opponent over any other player, including Mbappé's hero as a youngster, Cristiano Ronaldo. According to the CIES, Mbappé was the most expensive footballer in the world in 2018 in terms of the transfer value.

# MBAPPE VS. HAALAND

We now know where Kylian Mbappe and Erling Haaland, the two contenders for the title of finest player in the world, will play their football next season due to their signing new contracts with PSG and Manchester City, respectively.

By joining the Premier League champions-elect, Haaland's transfer will provide Pep Guardiola with more tools to use in his fight to win the Champions League.

Lifting the biggest trophy in Europe will be much easier said than done, though, since PSG will once again have access to one of the finest players in the world.

Who among Haaland and Mbappe, though, has a legitimate claim to being the GOAT in waiting?

Despite having started his career at Bryne, his parents' birthplace in Norway, the Norwegian striker Haaland was born in Leeds. Three months before turning 16, Haaland was forced into the main squad after scoring 18 goals in 14 games for Byrne's reserve team.

Despite not scoring in 16 games, Haaland performed well enough to transfer to Molde, a fellow Norwegian team. His influence on Molde was undoubtedly immediate because he scored in his debut. Haaland made 36 appearances in his debut season as a professional football player and scored four goals.

Mbappe was raised in Paris and played for AS Bondy as a youngster before joining the Clairefontaine academy, where he attracted the attention of the top teams in the world.

He chose to join AS Monaco and was initially going to play for their B team, but after just three weeks, he was quickly promoted to the main team.

Mbappe made his debut before turning 17 thanks to Leonardo Jardim, a year after Haaland. He broke Thierry Henry's previous record for being Monaco's youngest player.

He overtook Henry as the club's youngest goal scorer with his first for the team. Mbappe played 14 matches in his first season and scored once.

Haaland debuted over a year before Mbappe, although it was at a lower level, and he only became well-known when playing for Molde. Even then, he was signed up by the comparatively uncool Red Bull Salzburg.

Thierry Henry was written out of the Monaco record books by Mbappe, who won the Golden Boy title at 17. Mbappe also had the world's best teams vying for his signature. A simple victory for the Frenchman.

Focusing on numbers, Mbappe is 19 months older than Haaland, which should be mentioned.

Simply said, Kylian Mbappe has 226 goals in 335 appearances for club and nation as of May 20, 2022. It comes out to a goal being scored every 1.48 matches on average.

With 200 appearances and 150 goals, Haaland has participated in a great deal fewer games, or one every 1.33 games. The amount of penalties each player has scored from also equals 20, with Mbappe scoring 20 times from 12 yards and Haaland matching him.

Despite a few injuries this season, Haaland has played 30 times for Dortmund and scored 29 goals. Frenchman Kylian Mbappe had 45 appearances for PSG in 2021–2022, scoring 36 goals.

Haaland hasn't been scoring goals at the top level for as long as Mbappe has, thanks to his time spent at Monaco and PSG and his over 50 international appearances. Nevertheless, despite a hit-and-miss season, the Norwegian is scoring goals like crazy right now, which merely gives him the advantage. Mbappe has won 15 senior medals, including five Ligue 1 championships, and has done so more systematically. Mbappe scored in France's World Cup and Nations League championship games, helping his team to victory.

Haaland, in comparison, has only garnered four medals. These include three championships with the previous club Red Bull Salzburg and the DFB Pokal with current club Borussia Dortmund in 2021. (two Austrian Bundesliga and one Austrian Cup).

More precisely, when examining each club team's performance, Mbappe dominates in terms of assists, with 105 to Haaland's 36. (although the Norwegian has played almost 100 fewer games).

Mbappe, who can play in any offensive position and isn't just a striker, is seen as a forward player in modern football. Mbappe has played almost half his club games as a striker, with the remaining games seeing him either on the left or right side of the field. This highlights Mbappe's ability to innovate.

Haaland, on the other hand, is unquestionably No. 9. He can connect plays and is expected to finish in the 18-yard box, relieving him of the responsibility of providing assists.

Given his superior statistics in terms of both titles won and assists compared to Haaland, Mbappe emerges as the winner in this group. Haaland is a striker and is not anticipated to have as many assists on his resume. Still, given his young age, Mbappe's contributions to his teams at the club and international levels are laughable.

Football is entirely about marketability, despite how much we may not like to accept it. Early in the new millennium, Lionel Messi and Cristiano Ronaldo were perhaps more marketable stars than David Beckham was. But who will succeed them in the future?

Mbappe has already achieved greatness after having his image appear on the cover of FIFA 21 and signing a sponsorship agreement with Nike that is reportedly worth more than $10 million annually.

Haaland only has 15.7 million Instagram followers, but the Frenchman has 71 million.

Early in 2022, Nike's sponsorship with Haaland came to an end. He reportedly had a deal with Puma, a rival sports company, for approximately £7 million a year, but he chose Adidas instead. The Haaland camp requested £42 million spread over five years, although the agreement's specifics are yet unknown.

Without discussing their FIFA ratings, we cannot compare the two, allowing us to contrast them with Messi and Ronaldo.

The top-rated player in FIFA 22 is PSG's Messi, who has a rating of 93, while Ronaldo has a rating of 91. Mbappe, a teammate of Messi, has a rating of 91, indicating that the time for a new guard is rapidly approaching.

Given that he is only 21 years old, Haaland received a rating of 88 this year, which is amazing.

Looking more closely at the statistics, Mbappe outpaces Haaland in pace (97-89), making him the game's quickest player ahead of Adama Traore (96).

The Norwegian striker wins the shooting contest (91-88) and has an advantage in defence (45-36).

Mbappe has outstanding dribbling abilities and a passing grade of 15 more than Haaland, according to his stats in the 90s (92).

Given that he stands at 6 feet 4 inches (1.94 meters), Haaland dominates the physical category, outperforming Mbappe's base card's 77 with a score of 88.

## MADRID BOUND?

Kylian Mbappe claimed that Paris Saint-"sporting Germain's project," not money, persuaded him to reject Real Madrid and extend his contract with the French champions by three years.

The striker left the door open for a potential exit in 2025 when speaking at a press conference on Monday with PSG president Nasser Al-Khelaifi. He also denied having conversations about his desire to have more influence off the field.

Before their season-ending match against Metz at Parc des Princes, PSG announced on Saturday that Mbappe would be signing a new contract, ending one of the most publicized transfer sagas in recent memory.

"Everyone is aware that last year, I wanted to go. However, things have changed individually and in the world of sports, "said Mbappe. "It wasn't the correct decision to leave my nation. This has an emotional component, and the sports endeavour has also evolved. We discussed the athletic endeavour for months, but we only briefly discussed money."

After days of doubt over his future, the 23-year-old reportedly personally visited Madrid president Florentino Perez on Saturday to announce his U-turn.

Mbappe stated, "I made my decision last week. "Florentino Perez and I chatted. I have a great deal of admiration for him and Real Madrid. They went above and above to get me there and make me happy, and I appreciate that."

Mbappe has been a longtime goal of Real Madrid, and the club has come close to signing him numerous times, most recently last summer when they made several offers totalling up to €200 million to take advantage of his current contract.

Madrid maintained contact with Mbappe's team throughout this season and thought they had the player's word that he would join them once his contract expired on June 30.

To convince him to stay in Paris, the attacker disputed that PSG had given him the club leadership and involvement in transfer strategy and other important choices.

He said, "I'm not going to go above and beyond my position as a player. "No specific authority is required for you to participate in this initiative. I'm not trying to replace Marquinhos as captain of this team; he already holds that position. I don't have to be the captain to express my opinion."

Mbappe, born and raised in Paris, has been at PSG for five years and has amassed 171 goals, including a hat-trick in Saturday's 5-0 victory against Metz, becoming him the club's second-highest scorer of all time.

But when asked if he planned to stay at the club until 2025, Mbappe wouldn't rule out leaving on Monday.

He remarked, "You should look forward, but not too far ahead. That's something I learned in football." "I never imagined I'd be in this position a year ago, and now that I've signed a new deal, I'm concentrating on this new project. What will transpire in the future is unknown to me. In three years, I don't know where I'll be."

# PERSONAL LIFE

Mbappé discussed his adolescent sacrifices for his football growth in a 2018 interview with Time, saying, "I did not have the moments of so-called normal people during adolescence, like going out with friends, enjoying nice times." However, Mbappé claims that despite losing out on a "normal" existence, he is "living the life he always dreamed of." After making his professional debut just over four years prior, he had amassed over 50 million Instagram followers. Although he acknowledges that after initially coming to public attention, his "life has been utterly flipped upside down," he claims to be "glad."

Ethan Kylian, the brother of Kylian, signed an "aspiring" contract on June 25, 2021, with Paris Saint-Germain that would extend until 2024.

Nike, a provider of athletic apparel and equipment, endorses Mbappé. At 18, Nike released the Kylian Mbappé Nike Hypervenom 3 football footwear in recognition of his extraordinary skill. He revealed the Nike Mercurial Superfly VI boots in 2018, modelled by Ronaldo's R9 Mercurial boots during his time as a Brazilian striker. Hublot, a Swiss wristwatch, appointed Mbappé as a worldwide ambassador in 2018.

His younger brother Ethan, who would do the same while defeating Kylian at FIFA, served as the inspiration for his signature goal celebration, which entails standing with his arms crossed and hands tucked under his armpits. In FIFA 19, the celebration may be seen. Mbappé is the youngest person on the cover alone of FIFA 21 and is featured as the game's cover star. He was one of the few players to appear on the FIFA 22 cover for the second year in a row, making him a rare player.

In a meeting with French President Emmanuel Macron and FIFA President Gianni Infantino at the Élysée Palace in Paris on February 22, 2018, Mbappé was joined by two of Africa's greatest strikers, former AC Milan forward and current Liberia President George Weah and former Chelsea and Ivory Coast forward Didier Drogba. The meeting focused on a project for sports development in Africa. Mbappé claimed that because his parents are of African descent, he cares deeply about the growth of African sports.

A crowdfunding effort to support a private search operation to find football player Emiliano Sala, whose light aircraft had vanished over the English Channel a week earlier, received a $34,000 (about £26,000) donation from Mbappé on January 28, 2019.

Later, on February 10, 2019, Mbappé contributed an additional £27,000 to the GoFundMe effort to finance the hunt for the aircraft's still-missing pilot, David Ibbotson.

Mbappé and Zhang Jiaqi, who won the gold medal in diving for China at the 2020 Summer Olympics, served as godparents to two young pandas on November 19, 2021, at the Beauval Zoo in Paris as part of a campaign to raise awareness of the endangered species.

Mbappe, who is already a world champion and a two-time league champion, is now aiming to add Champions League gold to his impressive resume. Mbappe is superior to other young players on the PSG team because he prefers to play video games on TV rather than go out clubbing and waste money.

Even his distinctive goal celebration pays homage to Ethan, his younger brother, who would do the hands-under-the-arms move anytime he defeated his well-known older sibling in FIFA video games.

He is still as grounded as ever.

While Messi and Ronaldo have recently dominated the individual awards, Mbappe is expected to continue to be one of the sport's most renowned players for a long time.

He is unquestionably unique. After facing Mbappe and France in late 2018, Icelandic star Johan Berg Gudmundsson said, "He is the fastest player I have ever seen play, and I have played against Ronaldo and Messi."

The fact that he is so young and what he has accomplished in the past years is remarkable. He has already accomplished a great deal. As long as he keeps his head straight and maintains his humility, he will eventually become the finest player in the world.

For Mbappe, everything has so far gone according to plan. "I won't let anything distract me since I know what I want to achieve and where I want to go."

Due to his exceptional technical, athletic, and cerebral attributes, Mbappe is undoubtedly the most promising player in the world among players his age, claimed PSG president Nasser Al-Khelaifi upon Mbappe's signing with the capital club.

Since making a name for himself at the top level, he has developed a stellar reputation as an extremely mature, open, and courteous young star.

A football player worth €180 million. a World Cup champion. The scorer of 84 goals for the senior team, including more than 10 goals for France and four goals in that glorious World Cup victory. A 3-time Ligue 1 champion, first with Monaco and subsequently with PSG.

Such a list of accomplishments would be more than enough to please most professional football players for the duration of their entire careers. Mbappe, fueled by ambition and tenacity, is only getting started. And he keeps his feet firmly planted on the earth.

## What Did You Think?

First of all, thank you for purchasing this book. We know you could have picked any number of books to read, but you picked this book and for that, we are extremely grateful.

If you enjoyed this book and found some benefit in reading this, we'd love to hear from you and hope that you could take some time to post a review on Amazon. Your feedback and support will help us to know what you like.

Once again from the entire 'My Football Hero' family, thank you!

## REFERENCES

- "Kylian Mbappé: Profile". *worldfootball.net*. HEIM:SPIEL.
- "Kylian Mbappé: Overview". ESPN.
- "Kylian Mbappé". Paris Saint-Germain F.C.
- "Kylian Mbappe: LaLiga criticizes 'scandalous' deal to make PSG star world's highest-paid footballer."
- "PSG trigger Kylian Mbappe's permanent transfer from Monaco." ESPN. 19 February 2018.
- "Kylian Mbappé." *L'Équipe* (in French). Paris.
- Laurens, Julien (15 April 2020). "Ready to take over from Messi and Ronaldo? Why could Kylian Mbappe define the next era of football". *FourFourTwo*.
- "Qui est la mère de Mbappé ? L'Algérienne originaire de Kabylie ?" [Who is the mother of Mbappé? The Algerian originally from Kabylia?].

- Kindzeka, Moki Edwin. "Cameroon Football Fans Cheer for French Player with Ties to Africa." Voice of America.
- "Kylian Mbappe: How France World Cup star rose to prominence." *BBC Sport.*
- "Brother of PSG star scores on his debut." Pulse.
- "Mbappe after red card: I would do it again." *FourFourTwo.*
- Johnson, Jonathan (2 September 2018). "PSG's Kylian Mbappe doesn't regret red card: 'I would do the same thing.'" ESPN.
- "Mbappe breaks 45-year Ligue 1 record in PSG rout". *Goal.com.* Perform Group.
- Aarons, Ed (4 December 2018). "Ada Hegerberg: first women's Ballon d'Or marred as the winner is asked to twerk." *The Guardian.*
- "Paris St-Germain 9–0 Guingamp". *BBC Sport.*
- "Man. United 0–2 Paris". UEFA.
- "Caen 1–2 Paris Saint Germain". *BBC Sport.*
- "Paris 1–3 Man. United". UEFA.
- "Mbappe nets hat trick, Neymar returns as PSG beat Monaco on title-clinching day." *ESPN*. G make Ligue 1 history despite defeat". *Fox Sports Asia.* 24 May 2019.
- "Mbappé wins awards double". Ligue 1.

Made in the USA
Las Vegas, NV
29 December 2022

64411856R00059